DATE DUE	
JUL 0 9 2010		
JUL 1 9 2010		MAR 1 7 2013
AUG 2 3 2010		
APR 2 3 2011		
SEP 2 0 2011		
DEC 1 3 2011	FEB 12 2013	

GLOBAL WARMING

SEYMOUR SIMON

Smithsonian | Collins
An Imprint of HarperCollinsPublishers

PHOTO CREDITS: page 2: © Image Plan/Corbis; page 3: © Bloomimage/Corbis; pages 4–5: © Warren Faidley/Corbis; page 7: visibleearth.nasa.gov; page 8: © Mike Powell/Getty Images; page 10: © J. Walker/Photo Researchers, Inc.; page 11: © Novastock/ Photo Researchers, Inc.; pages 12–13: © Bernhard Edmaier/Photo Researchers, Inc.; page 14: © Dan Guravich/Corbis; page 16: © Gregory G. Dimijian, M.D./Photo Researchers, Inc.; page 17: © Gregory G. Dimijian, M.D./Photo Researchers, Inc.; page 18: © Corbis; page 19: © Imaginechina/Yin enbiao/AP Images; page 21, top: © Alexis Rosenfeld /Photo Researchers, Inc.; bottom: © Georgette Douwma/Photo Researchers, Inc.; page 22: © Jean-Paul Nacivet/Getty Images; page 25: © Corbis Photography/Veer; page 26: © Martin Bond/Photo Researchers, Inc.; page 27: © Martin Bond/Photo Researchers, Inc.; page 28: © AP Images/Jerome Favre; page 29: © Unlisted Images, Inc.; page 30: © moodboard/Corbis; page 31: © Bloomimage/Corbis.

Library of Congress Cataloging-in-Publication Data

Simon, Seymour.
  Global warming / Seymour Simon. — 1st ed.
    p. cm.
  ISBN 978-0-06-114250-5 (trade bdg.) — ISBN 978-0-06-114251-2 (lib. bdg.)
  1. Global warming—Juvenile literature. I. Title.
QC981.8.G56S5498 2010
363.738'74—dc22

2009001265
CIP
AC

10 11 12 13 14   SCP   10 9 8 7 6 5 4 3 2 1
❖
First Edition

For Liz, with joy and happiness

Smithsonian Mission Statement

For more than 160 years, the Smithsonian has remained true to its mission, "the increase and diffusion of knowledge." Today the Smithsonian is not only the world's largest provider of museum experiences supported by authoritative scholarship in science, history, and the arts but also an international leader in scientific research and exploration. The Smithsonian offers the world a picture of America, and America a picture of the world.

Thousands of years ago, large parts of the land mass on Earth were covered by ice. The end of this ice age occurred about 11,000 years ago. Since then, Earth has been getting warmer. In recent decades, the rise in average temperature has been particularly rapid. "Global warming" is the term that has been used to describe these changes.

Weather and climate are different. Weather is what happens every day. Climate is the average weather over a period of years. For example, it's possible that the weather on any day might be cool but the average weather, the climate, is getting warmer.

Why is the climate changing? Could Earth be getting warmer by itself? Are people doing things that make the climate warmer? What will be the impact of global warming? Can we do anything about it?

Global warming is happening because of the greenhouse effect. A greenhouse is a house made of glass. The glass lets in sunlight but keeps warm air from escaping. Earth is not a greenhouse, but certain gases in the atmosphere act like the glass in a greenhouse. Sunlight passes through Earth's atmosphere and warms the ground. Some of the heat bounces back into space, but much of it remains trapped near the ground by carbon dioxide, water vapor, and other greenhouse gases in the atmosphere.

The greenhouse effect helps make Earth warm enough for life to exist. But if greenhouse gases are released into the atmosphere in larger amounts much faster than before, then the warming will get much stronger and the climate will noticeably change.

In 2007, a report by 2,500 scientists from 130 countries concluded that humans are responsible for much of the current warming. No *one* person causes global warming. But there are billions of people on Earth. We cut down huge numbers of trees, drive hundreds of millions of cars and trucks, and burn vast amounts of coal and oil. All these activities contribute to a huge increase in greenhouse gases. Even if we decreased the amount of gases we now produce, it would not immediately stop the warming because greenhouse gases stay in the atmosphere for years.

The Earth's climate is very complex, and many factors play important roles in determining how the climate changes. Natural variations in Earth's orbit around the sun change the amount of sunlight we receive and thus the temperature. Earth has had much warmer and much colder climates in the distant past.

Most scientists agree that something different is happening now. While Earth's climate has always varied, it is now changing more rapidly than in any other time in recent centuries. Since we have been keeping weather records, nineteen of the twenty hottest years *ever* have happened since 1980.

For thousands of years, the balance of greenhouse gases in the atmosphere had not changed much. But now we burn huge amounts of coal, oil, and natural gas to generate energy. Every year, billions of tons of carbon dioxide pour out from the exhausts of cars, trains, trucks, airplanes, buses, and ships and from the chimneys of factories. There is 30 percent more carbon dioxide in the air than there was 150 years ago.

Trees, like other green plants, convert carbon dioxide into oxygen.

But trees and forests are cut down in huge numbers. When wood burns or decays, even more carbon dioxide is released. Carbon dioxide enters into the atmosphere much faster than the remaining forests and oceans can absorb it.

The release of other greenhouse gases adds to the speed at which the world's climate is changing. Methane is released by millions and millions of cattle and other farm animals. Nitrous oxide comes from chemicals used in soil fertilizers, as well as from automobiles.

The Arctic is already showing the effects of global warming. Average temperatures in the northern regions of Alaska, Canada, and Russia have risen twice as fast as in the rest of the world. The Ward Hunt Ice Shelf, the largest single sheet of ice in the Arctic, has been around for 3,000 years. It started to crack in 2000. By 2002, it had split. Now it is breaking into smaller pieces.

The Arctic Ocean is the great body of sea ice that covers the North Pole. Satellite photographs show that the ice pack has been shrinking and thinning in depth since the early 1990s. Scientists say that for the first time in human history, ice may disappear from the Arctic Ocean every summer.

Global warming has also changed the feeding patterns and behaviors of polar bears, walruses, seals, and whales. It may even impact their survival.

Polar bears live only in the Arctic. They are completely dependent on the sea ice for all their life needs. In the winter, females give birth to cubs. The mother polar bear eats little or no food during the winter.

As spring approaches, the bear family makes a run onto the sea ice to feed on seals, their main source of food. If the ice melts, their food supply will be cut off and this will impact their survival.

Grinnell and Salamander
Glaciers, 1957

Glaciers and mountain snow covers are rapidly melting. Almost every glacier in Alaska is receding. A few decades ago, huge rivers of ice stretched over the land. Now hundreds of feet or sometimes miles of bare rock and soil are exposed. In 1963, the Mendenhall Glacier Visitor Center in Juneau opened, very close to the glacier. Today, it is a mile or more away from the frozen edge of the retreating glacier.

In the 1850s, there were 150 glaciers in Montana. By 1968, there were 37. In 2008, there were fewer than 24. Glaciers that have lasted for thousands of years may be gone in two decades.

The icy coverings on tall mountain peaks are also disappearing. Each year, there is less snow remaining on the mountains during the summer. The snow melts earlier by a week or more in the spring, and snow falls later by a week or more in the autumn.

Grinnell and Salamander
Glaciers, 2004

As temperatures rise, the level of the oceans will rise. A recent study found that if average temperatures rise by 3° Celsius (5.4° Fahrenheit), Greenland's enormous ice sheet will begin to melt and sea levels all over the world may rise by a half foot to 3 feet or more.

This may happen over years or decades or may take longer than a century. A 3-foot rise in sea level would swamp the Gulf Coast and every East Coast city from Boston to Miami. Rising waters would cover low-lying areas such as the Nile Delta and countries such as Bangladesh. Millions of people would be forced to move.

The Antarctic ice cap holds about 90 percent of the world's ice and about 70 percent of its freshwater. It does not look as if the entire ice cap will melt anytime soon, but if it does happen, sea levels would rise 20 or more feet. Now, *that* would cause major flooding in coastal areas.

Atmospheric warming can cause a rise in ocean temperatures and place coral reefs in jeopardy. Coral reefs are huge branching structures made of the limestone skeletons of tiny animals called coral polyps. Coral reefs are found in warm, clear, shallow oceans. They are home to many kinds of fishes, jellyfish, anemones, crabs, turtles, sea snakes, clams, and octopuses and the algae that give the reefs their stunning colors.

Most coral reefs are highly sensitive. Even small changes in water temperature and in the amount of carbon dioxide in the water can kill algae in a reef. When the coral dies, it bleaches white. In 1998, a weather pattern called El Niño warmed the seas. In just one year, about one in every six of the world's reefs was lost. If coral reefs die, then much of the animal life they support will be wiped out as well.

Changing climate affects every ocean and every continent. Rising temperatures add heat energy and water vapor to the atmosphere. That can lead to heavier rainfalls and more powerful storms in some places, and long droughts in others. The changes will differ depending upon the location.

Many tropical areas may have greater rainfall. But in dry regions, even less rain may fall. Higher temperatures will cause the soil to dry up, and terrible droughts may ensue.

Wildfires may increase in forested areas as timberlands grow drier. The fires are likely to be bigger and more frequent and to burn longer. They would also release more carbon dioxide into the atmosphere and could lead to more warming.

Climate changes are not as easy to notice as changes in the weather. For example, a particular storm or a number of warm days during a winter is not really evidence of anything. We can all see day-to-day weather changes. But climate changes are noticeable as well. Plants and animals are already showing the effects of Earth's warming. Cold places, such as the North and South Poles and mountaintops, have been the first to feel the heat. Spring has come earlier, the ice has melted sooner, and there are fewer days where the temperatures are below freezing.

Many kinds of wildlife need the cold to survive. Some animals have adapted to the warmer weather by migrating to colder places. As the climate has warmed over the past century, the colorful checkerspot butterfly of the American West has moved northward or to higher elevations. The checkerspot butterfly has almost completely disappeared from its original home in Mexico and has adjusted to its new northern home in Canada. But not every animal can travel as easily. Scientists worry that crowding on mountaintops and colder places will cause some species to become extinct.

Baltimore checkerspot butterflies

We can't do anything about some changes in our environment. Our planet may be going through a natural cycle of getting warmer. However, most scientists say that humans are at least partly responsible for climate change. That means it may be possible for people to slow down the change.

There is a debate about what we can do about our changing climate. Here's what people in some nations are trying to do:

- ➤ Improve fuel and energy economy so that people use less energy for vehicles, schools, offices, homes, and factories.

- ➤ Encourage the use of wind and solar power.

- ➤ Explore alternative ways of producing energies that do not directly release more greenhouse gases into the atmosphere.

- ➤ Protect and plant trees to increase forestlands.

Nations and governments can do certain things to slow down dramatic climate changes. People can help, too. They can choose to use less energy to heat and cool their houses or use less fuel when getting around. Here are some things we might consider:

- Walking, biking, or using public transportation. One school bus can carry the same number of children as 30 or more cars.

- Using sturdy reusable bags for shopping and reusable cups and glasses is less wasteful than using disposable bags and cups.

- Taking short showers uses less energy than long showers.

- Planting a single tree can make enough oxygen for the lifetimes of two people. If one million trees are planted, the trees would eventually absorb more than one million tons of carbon dioxide.

Here's what some families are doing to slow down rapid climate change:

➤ Using fans instead of air conditioners. They may set a house air conditioner slightly higher in the summer, and slightly lower their heaters. They may lower a water heater's thermostat from "hot" (about 135° F.) to "warm" (about 120° F.).

➤ Using energy-saving fluorescent lightbulbs instead of incandescent lightbulbs. Fluorescent lightbulbs are more energy efficient and save on electricity costs.

➤ Turning off electric appliances and lights when they are not being used.

➤ Installing double-paned windows, extra insulation, good weather stripping, and solar panels to houses also saves energy.

Global warming isn't just about the Arctic Ocean melting and distant deserts becoming drier and hotter. Climate change impacts all of us. It can affect the world's food supply and the economic stability of countries.

The people and the governments of the world are developing the tools and the scientific know-how to meet these challenges. As Earth's climate continues to change, we all want to find ways to safeguard our own and future generations.

GLOSSARY

Atmosphere—A blanket of gases surrounding Earth or other planetary bodies that is held in place by gravitational forces.

Carbon dioxide—A colorless, odorless gas formed when a carbon-based fuel is burned, when a human or animal exhales during respiration, or during photosynthesis in plants.

Drought—An extended period of little to no rainfall that negatively affects plant and human life.

El Niño—A phenomenon that occurs every 4 to 12 years during winter months, in which the surface water of the Pacific Ocean around South America rises in temperature and affects weather patterns.

Fluorescent lightbulb—A source of light that is 4 to 6 times more efficient than a regular incandescent lightbulb. This saves on electricity while producing the same amount of light.

Glacier—A large mass of ice formed by the accumulation of packed snow that slowly moves downhill.

Greenhouse effect—A phenomenon that occurs when the sun's energy is trapped by Earth's atmosphere, producing temperatures that are warm enough to allow life to exist on Earth.

Greenhouse gases—Gases such as carbon dioxide, methane, nitrous oxide, and water vapor that contribute to the greenhouse effect.

Ice age—A cold period of time during which glaciers covered a large part of Earth's surface.

Ice sheet—A large sheet of ice and snow that covers a vast area of land, typically larger than 19,500 square miles.

Incandescent lightbulb—A source of electric light that works by heat-driven light emissions.

North Pole—The northernmost point on Earth.

Solar power—Energy from the sun that produces thermal or electrical energy.

South Pole—The southernmost point on Earth.

Timberlands—Forested land.

Wind power—Electricity or mechanical power that is provided by the wind.

INDEX

READ MORE ABOUT IT

Environmental Defense Fund
www.edf.org

Environmental Protection Agency Global Warming Site
www.epa.gov/climatechange

NASA
www.nasa.gov

National Wildlife Federation on Global Warming
www.nwf.org/globalwarming

Smithsonian Institution
www.si.edu